JESSE JACKSON
—A Biography—
Patricia C. McKissack

SCHOLASTIC INC.
New York Toronto London Auckland Sydney

PHOTO CREDITS

FRONT COVER: J.L. Atlan/Sygma
BACK COVER: Jacques Chenet/Woodfin Camp & Associates, Inc.

pp. 5, 23, 31, 39, 46, 61, 62, 71, 72, 76, 87, UPI/Bettmann Newsphotos; pp. 7, 10, 12, 14, 97, Greenville Cultural Exchange Center; pp. 8, 43, 44, 49, 54, 55, 64, 69, 79, 81, 85, 94, 96, AP/Wide World Photos; p. 16, *The New York Times;* pp. 21, 22, 27, North Carolina A&T/University Studios; p. 29, Charles Moore/Black Star; p. 36, Bruce Anspach/EPA Newsphoto, Art Resources; pp. 89, 90; Robert Trippett/SIPA Press.

ISBN 0-590-42395-9

12 11 10 9 8 7 6   03 02 01 00

Printed in the U.S.A.   40

Contents

For Jim and Kathy

ACKNOWLEDGMENTS

Writing about Jesse Jackson has been a joy. The following people helped make it so, and I wish to express my sincere thanks to them all, especially but not limited to the following: my editor, Ann Reit, and staff; my husband and partner, Fredrick McKissack; Ruth Ann Butler at the Greenville Cultural Exchange Center; Inez Lyons, archivist at the North Carolina A&T State University Library; Otis Harrington at University Studios in Greensboro, N.C.; Mabel Walker at Operation PUSH; and a special thanks to Mrs. Jacqueline Jackson for providing requested information about the Jackson children.

Prologue:
The Victory

The polling places have closed. The 1988 Michigan primary election is over. Everybody expects Vice President George Bush will win the Republican contest. But the whole country is anxiously awaiting the Democrats' results.

Six major candidates have been actively seeking the Democratic party's nomination for president of the United States. One particular man has been getting a lot of attention. He has been a political leader for many years. He speaks well, he is knowledgeable, and is well respected. He has met with more world leaders than any of his opponents. The polls show that among the Democratic primary candidates, he is the most recognizable.

But something is different about this particular candidate. He is an African-American. Some political analysts call him a "black candidate" running for the presidency of "black America." They insist that he is "unelectable," because the United States is not ready for a black president. Whites will not vote for him.

But forty-six-year-old Jesse Louis Jackson doesn't think so. "To say that a white person will not vote for me because I am black is essentially to say that he or she is so warped that they are incapable of voting their own interests. I don't believe that."

By late evening Jackson's confidence in the American voter is rewarded. He wins the Michigan Democratic primary. It is a victory for him and America. Jackson's win shows that inner city blacks and suburban whites can rise above racial prejudices. Jackson praises Michigan voters. This victory proves that he is a legitimate candidate for president of the United States.

But before that victorious day in Michigan, Rev. Jesse Louis Jackson had traveled a long and winding road. It began in Greenville, South Carolina, in the year 1941.

1
Growing Up in Greenville

There is a very good reason why Jesse Jackson says, "No child should be called *illegitimate*." He understands how painful it is to be so labeled. "All life is legitimate," he adds with a set jaw and flashing dark eyes. Inside this man there is the story of a little boy who was born with two strikes against him: He was black and his mother was not married to his father.

Helen Burns, a seventeen-year-old high school junior, knew her pregnancy was going to create a terrible scandal. Living next door to Noah Robinson, the baby's father, who was already married, made matters worse. In a small town like Greenville, South Carolina, having a baby out of wedlock placed a terrible burden on both mother and child.

The baby was unplanned, but it was not unwanted. Helen endured the harsh gossip, and on October 8, 1941, she gave birth to a seven-pound, four-ounce boy. She named her son Jesse Louis Burns, after Noah's father, Jesse Louis Robinson.

Helen loved the bright-eyed baby. He was beautiful and full of energy. His father loved him, too. The midwife who delivered him said, "It seemed that the child was in a hurry to get there."

When Jesse was two years old, his mother married Charles Jackson, who made his living as a postal worker. Mr. Jackson often stated proudly, "We were never poor. We never wanted for anything. We've never been on welfare because I was never without a job. We never begged anybody for a dime. And my family never went hungry a day in their lives."

Jesse's mother supplemented the family income by running a beauty shop in her house.

For years Jesse grew up believing Charles Jackson was his real father. Nobody ever told him otherwise. "I didn't want him to grow up thinking he was different," said Mr. Jackson.

Different was a word most black children in the South associated with negative feelings. Blacks and whites were not the same, the most obvious difference being the way black people were treated. Strict laws forced the races to live apart. They could not go to school together, eat together, or go to a movie together. As a way of coping, Jesse said, "We would say we didn't want to eat because we weren't hungry; or we didn't want to drink water because we weren't thirsty; or we

Sign outside the waiting room of the Illinois Central Railroad Station in Jackson, Mississippi, 1962.

didn't want to go to the movie theater because we didn't want to see the picture. Actually, we were lying because we were afraid."

All his life Jesse questioned segregation, asking, for example, why he had to walk five miles to Nicholtown Elementary when there was a school two blocks away. That's the way things are, he was told. The system was unfair, and Jesse was quick to express his feelings. He was warned not to be so outspoken. Challenging white people could be dangerous. Young Jesse would soon learn just how dangerous.

One day he went into the neighborhood store where all the children bought candy. The white store owner was busy talking and ignored the boy. Jesse impatiently whistled for help. Suddenly a gun was pointed in his face. "Don't you ever whistle at a white man again as long as you live," the store owner spoke angrily. There was no doubt in Jesse's mind that the store owner meant what he said. That is how young black children were taught to stay "in their place." The ever-present threat of punishment and even death kept them from "getting out of line."

Being different in the South meant feeling inferior. But Jesse's grandmother, Matilda Burns, was determined not to let anything cripple her grandson's spirit.

"You're as good as the next person, and don't you forget it," she told him over and over. Although she could not read or write, her words were wise and good. "Promise me you'll be somebody," she whispered to the child. "Nobody's going to think much of you unless you think so yourself."

Jesse loved his grandmother very much. He called her Grandmother Tibby, and living up to her expectations was always important to him. "Idle hands are the devil's workshop," she said. So from age six he held a job of some kind — helping cut firewood, selling snacks at football games, shining shoes, and working in a bakery. Whatever chore he set out to do, he did it well, because Grandmother Tibby always said, "If it's worth doing, then it's worth doing well."

Jesse Jackson with his mother, Helen, (left) and his grandmother, Matilda Burns, (right) at the Greenville Cultural Exchange Center, November 9, 1987.

Without question, Grandmother Tibby was a powerful force in Jesse's life, but the church had its influence, too. Praying was as much a part of his growing up as playing. When he was nine years old, he was chosen to attend the National Sunday School convention in Charlotte, North Carolina.

On Sunday mornings, he loved listening to joyful gospel songs and prayers of praise and thanksgiving. He especially liked the preacher's colorful and rhythmic language. One memorable Christmas, he got a chance to speak from the pulpit. It felt good and natural standing before the congre-

7

gation. He would never forget the inner calm and joy he felt.

Jesse got into his fair share of boyish scrapes, too. But he liked outsmarting his opponents with language rather than with his fists. Nothing was more exciting than winning a good verbal battle. "He was a great signifier, good at out-insulting those who thought they could insult him," a friend said.

With a loving and supportive family surrounding him, Jesse grew up feeling good about himself. Yet there was a nagging thought that bothered

As a young boy, Jesse did not dream that in June 1969, he would receive an honorary degree of Doctor of Divinity from the Chicago Theological Seminary.

him, and it had something to do with Noah Robinson.

Jesse knew Noah Robinson to be a man who gave respect but demanded it in return. Whites and blacks addressed him as Mr. Robinson during a time when blacks were generally called by their first names. He didn't duck or hide when white men drove through the community in trucks, demanding rent payments. He was a textile worker who moonlighted as a taxi driver. Robinson was strong, handsome, and proud.

Then, quite by accident, Jesse learned the truth. He was perhaps nine or ten years old when his half-brother, Noah Robinson, Jr., told him they shared the same father. Jesse was confused, hurt, and surprised. Noah Robinson was his father? What about Charles Jackson? Jesse felt betrayed. Why hadn't he been told? The boy didn't know what to do with the knowledge. It took a long time for him to sort it all out.

Once Jesse knew, Noah took full responsibility for his son, never denying him, bragging proudly, "That's my boy. See, he looks just like me." Naturally, Noah, Jr., was jealous of Jesse. And sometimes Jesse felt left out of his real father's life. To compensate for it, Jesse excelled at whatever he tried. Anybody would have been proud to call him son.

His high school French teacher remembered him as a student who "never complained, never made excuses for himself, never wallowed in self-pity."

*In 1959,
in Jesse's senior year
at Sterling High,
he and
Willie June Thompson
were elected the
best athletes
of the year.*

   High school students remember calling him The
Filibusterer. When they wanted to distract a
teacher from class lessons, they got Jesse to talk.
   As a young teen, Jesse was handsome, popular
with the girls, an honor student, class officer, and
star athlete. Yet there was an overwhelming feeling inside himself. Being good wasn't enough for
him. He worked hard at being the best — number
one. And most of the time he was.

2
Separate and Unequal

Jesse was a scholar-athlete who earned letters in football, basketball, and baseball. Coach J. D. Mathis rated him one of the best high school quarterbacks he'd ever coached, describing Sterling High's gridiron star as "a fierce competitor," one who "could take a punch and then dish out a blow. . . ."

Jesse also distinguished himself in baseball. For a high school player, he had a strong arm, an accurate eye, and amazing versatility on the mound. Zinging fast balls over the plate with unusual speed and control, the young hurler caught the eye of several major league recruiters. After graduating in 1959, Jesse was offered a chance to try out for the New York Giants. The Chicago White Sox were also interested in signing him.

11

To an eighteen-year-old, playing in the majors was a dream come true — earning big money, buying all the things associated with success. Naturally Jesse was excited when a $6,000 contract offer arrived from the Giants. (At the time, teachers earned about $2,500 a year.) He wanted to sign and would have, except the same team offered

In 1958 Jesse was also an outstanding football player at Sterling High.

Dickie Dietz, another hometown ballplayer, $95,000 to sign on as a catcher. Why was Dietz offered so much more money? Jesse wondered. Sure, Deitz was a good player, but so was he. Why?

The answer was more perplexing than the question. *White men get paid more than black men for doing the same job. That's the way things are. Learn to live with it.*

It wasn't the first time Jesse had encountered racial discrimination; still it was no less painful or disappointing. Some people advised him to sign, saying it was a good offer — for a black man. But Jesse didn't think so. The deal was unfair, so he turned it down.

Besides, a football scholarship was waiting for him at the University of Illinois that fall. The opportunity to play quarterback for a Big Ten university wasn't a bad alternative. And race relations, he thought, would surely be less strained in the North. With the baseball incident behind him, Jesse arrived at the University of Illinois with renewed hope and high expectations.

Having always played quarterback, he expected to continue. However, an assistant coach bluntly explained that talented or not, blacks just didn't play quarterback. Ability had nothing to do with the decision. Jesse could play if he changed to a running position, but he resented the suggestion that a black athlete was incapable of leading a team to victory. Another dream was shattered.

Jesse was also disappointed with campus life. Going to school "up North" hadn't presented any

Photo at top shows Jesse (third from left) in 1958 as a member of the student council. Below, Jesse (far left) in his high school chemistry lab, 1958.

special social advantages. For the most part, black students clustered together and didn't participate in student activities outside the classroom.

Jesse explained the situation to one of his biographers, Barbara Reynolds. "The annual interfraternity dance was the social event of the fall, but the three black fraternities weren't invited . . . we were listening to recordings while the white folks were jumping live to Lionel Hampton in the gym." After many years, there is still a hint of anger in his words.

Jesse was thirteen years old in 1954 when the Supreme Court ruled that separate schools were unequal, and age sixteen during the Montgomery [Alabama] Bus Boycott. While Jesse was in Illinois, a new phase of the civil rights movement was beginning. Dramatic things were happening "down home," and Jesse watched with interest.

In North Carolina, a student-led civil rights movement was making headlines.

For years, Southern black shoppers had tolerated a system that permitted them to buy merchandise but would not allow them to buy a meal at the lunch counter in the same store. Prominently displayed signs announced that eating areas were reserved for *Whites Only*.

Tired of just talking about how bad things were, four black students at North Carolina Agricultural and Technical College in Greensboro decided to take action and challenge the system. They targeted the national F. W. Woolworth chain. On February 1, 1960, the students bought a few items,

"All the News That's Fit to Print"

The New York Times.

LATE CITY EDITION
Fair and cool today. Mostly sunny, continued cool tomorrow.

VOL. CIII...No. 35,176.

NEW YORK, TUESDAY, MAY 18, 1954.

FIVE CENTS

HIGH COURT BANS SCHOOL SEGREGATION; 9-TO-0 DECISION GRANTS TIME TO COMPLY

McCarthy Hearing Off a Week as Eisenhower Bars Report

SENATOR IS IRATE

President Orders Aides Not to Disclose Details of Top-Level Meeting

By W. H. LAWRENCE

Communist Arms Unloaded in Guatemala By Vessel From Polish Port, U. S. Learns

State Department Views News Gravely Because of Red Infiltration

REACTION OF SOUTH

'Breathing Spell' for Adjustment Tempers Region's Feelings

By JOHN N. POPHAM

Embassy Says Nation of Central America May Buy Munitions Anywhere

1896 RULING UPSET

'Separate but Equal' Doctrine Held Out of Place in Education

By LUTHER A. HUSTON

LEADERS IN SEGREGATION FIGHT

SOVIET BIDS VIENNA CEASE 'INTRIGUES'

Envoy Warns Austrian Chief on Inciting East Zone—Raab Denies Charges

By JOHN MacCORMAC

City Colleges' Board Can't Pick Chairman

2 TAX PROJECTS DIE IN ESTIMATE BOARD

Beer Levy and More Parking Collections Killed—Payroll Impost Still Weighed

By CHARLES G. BENNETT

MORETTI'S LAWYER MUST BARE TALKS

Jersey Court Orders Counsel to Racketeers in Bergen to Divulge Data to Grand Jury

By GEORGE CABLE WRIGHT

RULING TO FIGURE IN '54 CAMPAIGN

Decision Tied to Eisenhower—Russell Leads Southerners in Criticism of Court

By WILLIAM S. WHITE

INDO-CHINA PARLEY WEIGHS TWO PLANS

French and Rebel Peace Bids Will Be Studied Jointly as a Basis for Settlement

By THOMAS J. HAMILTON

Costello Is Sentenced to 5 Years, Fined $30,000 in U. S. Tax Case

By EDWARD RANZAL

Churchill Asks Negotiated Peace With Guarantees for Indo-China

By DREW MIDDLETON

Voice' Speaks in 34 Languages To Flash Court Ruling to World

Front page of The New York Times, *May 18, 1954.*

proceeded to the lunch counter, and ordered coffee. Service was denied, as was expected. The students politely stated they would *sit until served*. Thereafter, the *sit-in* became a part of our contemporary history and a symbol of the civil rights movement.

The unjust baseball contract and his year at the University of Illinois were experiences that added to Jesse's resentment of racial discrimination and peaked his political awareness. He wanted to be a part of the movement his generation was forming to get rid of unjust laws.

The following year, he gave up the athletic scholarship and transferred to North Carolina A&T. When Jesse Jackson arrived in Greensboro, the student sit-in movement was well underway. By 1964, however, he would be a principal leader.

3
The Call

Once enrolled at A&T, Jesse quickly moved into a leadership position, first joining the Congress of Racial Equality (CORE), the organization responsible for setting up the Greensboro demonstrations. Since the 1940s, CORE had worked for social change, but Jesse was dissatisfied with the local leaders and impatient with the slow progress. The impact of their monthly demonstrations was, for the most part, weak. Jesse complained so much and so long that he was given the job of organizing the various sit-ins. "Do better if you can!" the CORE leaders said. And he did.

Jesse energized the local student sit-in movement with his high-spirited personality. He intensified the demonstrations, holding them daily and involving hundreds of people. Always in the fore-front, he held *sleep-ins* at segregated hotels, or-ganized *watch-ins* at theaters, *eat-ins* at restau-rants, and *wade-ins* at swimming pools.

Some people were critical of Jackson's early leadership style, saying he was aggressive, ambi-tious and, at times, overbearing. Others described him as intense and flamboyant, but undeniably dedicated, determined, and daring. Perhaps there is a bit of accuracy in both points of view. While there might have been disagreement regarding his leadership style, the results of his efforts were ev-ident. Jesse got things done. People followed him because he was willing to lead.

Seemingly unafraid to face angry and abusive white opposition, Jackson earned the respect of his peers, teachers, and civil rights workers all over the state. And slowly Greensboro's racial barriers came down. Theaters, hotels, lunch counters, parks, and other public places were integrating.

Coming South had proved to be a good choice, for at A&T Jesse thrived as an athlete, a scholar, and a leader. He was a star quarterback, honor student, national vice grand president of Omega Phi Psi Fraternity, and student body president. By his senior year he was elected president of the newly formed North Carolina Intercollegiate Council on Human Rights.

In his whirlwind of activities, it seems impos-sible that Jesse could have had time to fall in love and marry. But he did.

During the sit-in movement, he met a Florida

beauty named Jacqueline Lavinia Davis — Jackie to all her friends. Jackie was a student at A&T and a very involved civil rights activist. She was a quiet person, bright, and well read. Unlike Jesse, who was quick to voice an opinion about everything, Jackie has been described as "the quiet rebel who thought more than she spoke."

The two became friends when Jackie discussed a term paper Jesse had written about whether Red China should be admitted to the United Nations. Jackie revealed later that she thought Jesse came to conclusions much too fast. Although they approached decision-making differently, they soon learned they had many more things in common. In time their friendship matured into love. In 1962, Jesse married Jackie at his parents' house in Greenville.

After graduating from A&T with a bachelor of science degree in sociology, the young civil rights worker considered enrolling in Duke University's law school. But inside he felt God had other plans for him. His roommate described Jesse's experience: "One night he woke up and said he had had an odd dream. He said that he thought he had been called to preach. He was shaking. I never saw him look so serious."

Since age fourteen, the idea of becoming a minister had been a shadowy thought. But even after the dream, he still had concerns. Was it possible to combine his spiritual beliefs and his political convictions?

Through his role models Jesse found an answer.

Jesse was a star quarterback at North Carolina Agricultural and Technical College in Greensboro.

At North Carolina A&T, Jesse (center) continued to be a leader in the student government.

The men he respected most were ordained ministers — men like Rev. James Hall, Dr. Sam Proctor, and Dr. Martin Luther King, Jr. — yet they were also social activists.

Rev. Hall, a Greenville pastor, had left a lasting impression on young Jesse. Rev. Hall had organized and led a demonstration protesting the treatment of Jackie Robinson at the Greenville airport restaurant. Robinson, the first black to play major league baseball, had been denied service, and Hall called attention to it, complaining that such treatment was an embarrassment to the city and an insult to all Americans. Robinson was a celebrated national hero who deserved better.

Historically, black churchmen had been leaders in the struggle for freedom and justice. Rev. Hall and others like him were the forerunners of Rev. Dr. Martin Luther King, Jr., who, by 1964, was the most important civil rights leader in the country. Jesse didn't know Dr. King at the time, but he admired his nonviolent approach to social change.

Jesse discussed his "call" with Dr. Sam Proctor, president of A&T, and a man whose opinion he valued. With Dr. Proctor's encouragement, he accepted a Rockefeller grant to attend Chicago Theological Seminary.

Having lived in the South all his life, Jesse was familiar with open racial discrimination. Northern

Students sitting-in at a Woolworth's lunch counter, demanding service, which they never received.

23

racism was more subtle, more difficult to detect, but the effects were just as shameful. In Chicago there were no social restrictions, no "for colored only" signs, no Jim Crow laws separating the races. But there were economic barriers that created a vast difference in the way whites and blacks lived. The nightmarish condition of Chicago's all-black neighborhoods surpassed any violence Jackson had experienced during the sit-ins in the South. Many years later he would call it "economic violence."

Whites controlled everything — politics, banks, law enforcement, education, property, and businesses — even in the ghetto. Most South Side housing was overcrowded, rat-infested, and in clear violation of city health and fire codes. Yet rents were high and maintenance slight. White-owned stores profited in the black community by charging ten to fifty percent more for goods and services. Unemployment was proportionately higher among black people than among white people, with unfair hiring and firing practices being contributory causes. Inadequate police protection left the streets open to crime and violence, and poorly equipped schools were cement jungles where failure was the standard.

Living in the ghetto was an endless cycle of poverty and despair passed from one generation to another with few avenues of escape. Jesse was saddened and angered by the overwhelming waste of human potential. Somehow the cycle had to be broken.

Although Jesse went to Chicago hoping to pursue his theological career in quiet, peaceful surroundings, he was hearing a call from beyond the seminary walls. It was a call that he could not ignore.

4
Working With Martin Luther King, Jr.

Although Jesse enjoyed his theological studies, he was happiest when working with people. Unsafe streets, poor housing and schools, high unemployment, and inadequate services were wrongs Jesse wanted to make right. So he joined the Chicago-based Coordinating Council of Community Organizations (CCCO), fifty religious, neighborhood, professional, and civic groups united to fight discrimination.

The Southern Christian Leadership Conference (SCLC) was headed by Rev. Dr. Martin Luther King, Jr. Headquartered in Atlanta, SCLC was the center of the civil rights movement. Jesse joined the Chicago chapter of SCLC because of his deep admiration for Dr. King's nonviolent approach to social change.

Jesse Jackson with the Rev. Dr. Martin Luther King, Jr.

Since the early 1960s, SCLC staff had been conducting peaceful protests such as marches, boycotts, and sit-ins. Slowly, racial barriers were coming down. Black and white people were eating together at lunch counters, riding buses and trains together, drinking from the same water fountains, and using the same building entrances. In 1965, these small advancements were considered big accomplishments.

Progress remained slow, and injustices still existed. For example, many Southern blacks could not vote because of unfair state laws. Dr. King and other civil rights leaders challenged these laws and sent workers into Southern towns to register black people to vote. There was a lot of resistance, especially in Mississippi and Alabama.

On March 7, 1965, SCLC organized a march from Selma, Alabama, to Montgomery, Alabama. The purpose was to let people know about the huge voter registration drive taking place and to urge passage of the Voting Rights Bill before Congress.

Alabama governor George Wallace didn't want the march to take place. He sent state troopers to stop it. When the marchers refused to turn back, the troopers used clubs, cattle prods, and tear gas. Hundreds of demonstrators, including Martin Luther King, Jr., were attacked and beaten.

Jesse, like other Americans, was shocked when he watched these cruel acts on television. He wondered how he might help. An answer came shortly. Dr. King promised to complete the march from Selma to Montgomery. He asked for help, and

Fire hoses were used to suppress civil rights demonstrators.

thousands of Americans responded. People came from the four corners of the nation — some riding, some walking. Those who could not walk were carried. Those who could not see were led. Rich and poor, young and old, blacks and whites came to show their support.

Jesse was part of that great effort. He brought a busload of seminary students to participate in the historic Selma-to-Montgomery March. His organizing ability impressed Rev. Dr. Ralph Abernathy, Dr. King's closest friend and advisor. Abernathy arranged for Jesse to meet with King.

In his usual take-charge manner, Jesse began

29

snapping orders and giving directions as though he were in charge. Those "in charge" were bothered by the young "upstart from Chicago." Andrew Young, who later became mayor of Atlanta, Georgia, was one of Dr. King's senior aides. He admitted that Jesse annoyed him. "But," Young recalled, "I also remember him telling me what a great pamphlet I had written. . . . I was flattered. . . . It sort of took the edge off."

Other SCLC aides were not impressed. They resented Jesse for giving orders, making unauthorized speeches, and taking every opportunity to be photographed with Dr. King. They questioned his motives, too. Was he honestly concerned? Or was he just being pushy and ambitious?

Barbara Reynolds, a Jackson biographer, has written: "Had Jesse been white, his peers would have labeled him 'promising, inspired, and diligent,' but a black with these same characteristics is often seen as 'uppity, audacious, and arrogant.'"

Other Jackson biographers have noted that all during the march Jesse had the ability to be wherever the cameras were. He was seen in picture after picture, standing near and sometimes right next to King, Abernathy, or Young. Since nobody questioned his presence, people began to accept him.

Betty Washington, a reporter for the *Chicago Daily Defender*, was curious when Jesse delivered a speech along with other top SCLC officials. "I thought it strange that he was making a speech when he was not on the SCLC staff. But he spoke well," says Washington. "I recorded his statement

30

anyway. I had the feeling that one day he might be important."

The Selma-to-Montgomery March ended with 50,000 marchers rallying at the state capitol. Afterwards, Jesse returned to Chicago. Congress passed the Voting Rights Bill, but peace was not in season.

The summer of 1965 was hot and steamy. Tempers clashed, and a minor incident set off the riots in Watts, a predominantly black section of Los Angeles. The California national guard was sent to control the fire bombings, looting, and violence. Another riot ripped through Chicago, followed by seven others in large cities. When all the penned-

Bedraggled freedom marchers as they begin the third day of the Selma-to-Montgomery March on March 23, 1965.

up anger and frustration were finally spent, parts of forty-three cities lay in smoldering ruins.

Al Raby, the director of the CCCO, invited Dr. Martin Luther King, Jr., to Chicago, hoping that his nonviolent program might help. Dr. King was saddened by the rioting. He accepted. At a news conference it was announced that the focus would be housing — "The Campaign to End Slums."

Jesse was delighted, but Chicago's political, financial, and religious leaders stood solidly against King's involvement. Mayor Richard Daley led the opposition. He was outraged that Chicago had been singled out. He denied that segregation existed in *his* city. "Here we recognize every man regardless of race, national origin, or creed, and they are entitled to their rights as provided in the United States Constitution and the Constitution of Illinois."

Jesse pointed out that no laws stopped black persons from eating at lunch counters. But racism and prejudice stopped blacks from getting a job so that they could afford to buy lunch.

Not all black leaders were in favor of King's visit, however. Congressman William Dawson responded angrily, "Chicagoans know what's best for Chicagoans." King was called "a meddling outsider" and accused of "seeking glory."

Criticism did not stop King's plans. Jesse and the Chicago SCLC office worked at organizing the program. It was difficult getting the community to participate. Petty arguments and fear kept them splintered. Jesse argued and persuaded; he would not give up. Slowly, people became involved.

In July 1966, Jackson met Dr. King at O'Hare Airport. Over 60,000 people attended a rally followed by a nonviolent march through Chicago's business section. Unlike Governor Wallace during the Selma-to-Montgomery March, Mayor Daley did not put up any resistance. In fact, the mayor met with King and promised to push for better housing. Underneath, though, Mayor Daley was furious. He had no intention of cooperating.

While King was in Chicago, he and Jesse became good friends. King respected Jesse's hard work and ability. Jesse was full of energy and fresh ideas. But he was also full of surprises. Sometimes he didn't follow orders and spoke without consulting others. Dr. King dealt with him patiently, like a loving father.

There was a series of marches, sit-ins, and rent strikes, which led to a weak housing agreement. SCLC claimed a victory, but in reality no improvements were really expected. After months of conflict and struggle, enthusiasm fizzled out and people lost interest. Dr. King returned to Atlanta, but not before placing Jesse in charge of Operation Breadbasket, the economic arm of SCLC. At age twenty-four, he became the youngest SCLC staff member.

With a limited budget, no staff, no widespread community support, and no political strength, Jesse was expected to take on the powerful and ruthless Daley administration. It was a tough job, but Jesse loved it.

5
Operation Breadbasket

Jesse set up shop in the heart of Chicago's South Side. With a staff member from the seminary, he made plans for Breadbasket's future. He quickly decided that sit-ins and marches worked in some cases, but they had not gotten the best results in Chicago. The economic boycott might be more effective.

"We are the margin of profit of every major item produced in America, from General Motors to Kellogg's Corn Flakes," Jesse told an audience. "We should be fairly represented in the work force of these companies."

His strategy, simply stated, was to boycott businesses that underemployed blacks or refused to support black products. "Hit them where it hurts the most — in their pocketbooks. Then we'll get their attention," Jesse said.

The number of black employees was compared with the percentage of company sales in the black community. When the figures were clearly unbalanced, Breadbasket sent the company a written proposal listing demands and asking for policy changes. If the company refused to cooperate, Breadbasket called for a strike. Shoppers were asked to avoid buying goods or services from the company.

The first Breadbasket strike was against Country Delight Dairies. Although a large percentage of their customers lived in the inner city, less than ten blacks were employed in their 104 stores.

Jesse contacted the company, pointing out the problem and asking for a change in hiring practices. Management refused. Country Delight was boycotted.

Since dairy products spoil easily, the company felt the economic pinch within three days. They quickly signed an agreement. But it wasn't until forty-four blacks were *actually* hired that people began buying again.

Success guarantees success. After the first Breadbasket victory, volunteers poured into the office. South Siders no longer considered Jesse an outsider. As his support among the poor and underprivileged increased, Breadbasket's campaign grew stronger and bolder.

The Red Rooster, another grocery chain,

Jesse Jackson leads Operation Breadbasket picketing outside the national headquarters of the A&P in New York City.

charged high prices for spoiled food and bad service. A boycott eventually drove them out of business. The High-Low Food Chain opened 184 new jobs to avoid a lengthy boycott.

Up until that time, Jesse had not challenged a national company. A&P Grocery Stores, one of the largest supermarket chains in America, owned forty stores in Chicago's black neighborhoods. Yet all the workers were white. When approached, A&P management refused to negotiate. Jesse called for a boycott. The community response was overwhelming. Still, it was a long, hard battle because A&P was larger and stronger than smaller local companies.

Word of Breadbasket's struggle spread beyond Chicago, and black shoppers boycotted A&P stores in other cities. "Why should we pay our hard-earned money to be mistreated?" one boycotter said. Many agreed with him. White shoppers joined the boycott, too. It was the first effort of its kind.

A&P management could not hold out; their losses were too great. Within four weeks, they gave in. The supermarket chain hired hundreds of black workers, not just in Chicago, but nationwide. In addition, stores stocked products made by blacks, hired black contractors to help build new stores, and deposited money in minority-owned banks.

The A&P success gave Jesse national exposure as a civil rights leader. Within the first year, Breadbasket had signed agreements with over ten major corporations. A year later, fifteen new branches had opened in other cities. Hundreds of men and women were working in better jobs for better pay. Black banks increased their deposits from $5 million to $22 million. Even pest control was a target. "We have a monopoly on rats in the ghetto, and we're going to have a monopoly on killing them," Jesse told an audience who stood and cheered.

Since his appointment as director of Breadbasket, Jesse had been holding meetings at the seminary every Saturday at 9:00 A.M. But attendance at the meetings had grown, so they were moved to the Capitol Theater in downtown Chicago. People of all ages, professions, and social backgrounds sat side by side listening to a "natural born" preacher man. All who heard him recognized that he was a gifted speaker who could hold an audience spellbound with words that encouraged, inspired, and motivated.

Jesse was aware of changing attitudes taking place within the black community. African-Americans were proudly claiming their cultural past. Racial pride was reflected in art, music, drama, dance, and literature. Wearing African clothing was an expression of self-acceptance, and the full "Afro" hairstyle expressed their new concept of beauty. "Black is beautiful" was a popular slogan. So was "Black power!"

But older civil rights leaders were concerned about the growing number of militant youths who were disgusted by what they considered slow progress in the civil rights movement. With clenched

In 1972, with Rev. Ralph Abernathy at the Democratic National Convention, Jesse Jackson wearing an African dashiki and the full Afro hairstyle.

fists raised overhead, the youths shouted angry slogans.

Jesse tried to redirect their anger away from violence and build on pride, dignity, and self-worth. He wore a full "Afro" and dressed in stylish "dashikis," yet his language remained positive and always nonviolent. When others were saying, "Burn, Baby, Burn!" Jesse was shouting, "Learn, Baby, Learn."

It was during one of his Saturday morning programs that Jesse began the famous "I Am Somebody" chant:

> *"I am somebody.*
> *I may be poor,*
> *but I am somebody!*
> *I may be uneducated,*
> *I may be unskilled,*
> *but I am somebody!*
> *I may be on welfare,*
> *I may be prematurely pregnant,*
> *I may be on drugs,*
> *I may be victimized by racism,*
> *but I am somebody!*
> *Respect me. Protect me. Never neglect me.*
> *I am God's child."*

Those who have been led in this stirring choral response say it is a memorable experience.

Meanwhile, garbage workers went on strike in Memphis, Tennessee. An old friend asked Dr. King to help. What was supposed to be a peaceful demonstration turned into a riot. King fled the scene, trying to distance himself from the violence. The youth gangs would not cooperate. They were uncontrollable. "Burn, Baby, Burn!" they shouted. Dr. King was criticized by the media. He had no other choice — SCLC had to return and conduct a peaceful march. His life's work was in jeopardy.

Along with other SCLC staff members, Jesse reported to Memphis. He had no way of knowing how the coming events would change his life.

6
Dreamer of New Dreams

Jesse stood outside the Lorraine Motel in Memphis, talking to Solomon Jones, Dr. King's driver. It had rained the night before, so water puddles dotted the parking lot. The air was crisp and cool.

Jesse looked up as King and Abernathy came out of room 306. They were preparing to leave for dinner at a friend's house. No doubt, the speech Dr. King had given the night before was still fresh in everyone's mind.

"Like anybody," he had said, "I'd like to live a long life. Longevity has its place. But I'm not concerned about that now. I just want to do God's will. And He's allowed me to go to the mountain. And I've looked over, and I've seen the Promised Land. I may not get there with you, but I want you to know that we as a people will get to the Promised Land."

To many it sounded like a farewell speech. Did Dr. King feel something was going to happen to him? Many people believe he did.

Abernathy went back into the room to put on some after-shave lotion. Dr. King spoke to several people, including Jesse. "Jesse, I want you to go to dinner with us tonight," he said. Then smiling he added, "And no blue jeans, all right?"

Jesse smiled. He was wearing a brown sweater and slacks. "Right, Doc," he answered.

April 3, 1968, the day before Dr. Martin Luther King, Jr., was assassinated. From left to right, Dr. Hosea Williams, Jesse Jackson, Dr. King, and the Rev. Ralph Abernathy.

King turned toward Abernathy, who was coming out of the door, when suddenly a loud crack echoed through the air. Everybody knew it was a gunshot, so they fell to the ground. Someone screamed. At the same time, Abernathy shouted that King had been shot. The rest is history. Rev. Dr. Martin Luther King, Jr., was pronounced dead on April 4, 1968, at 7:05 P.M. in Memphis, Tennessee.

Violence paralyzed cities from coast to coast. It was a sad good-bye to a man who believed in peace. The SCLC staff had agreed not to speak with

Following the shooting of Dr. King, people near the body point to the rooftop from where the shots seemed to have come.

the press. But Jesse did speak. The next day, he was back in Chicago, appearing on the *Today* show. SCLC members were shocked and angry.

Chauncey Eskridge, attorney for Dr. King, stated, "I thought it was ironic. Here we were, prepared to go get King's body from the funeral home — the whole staff — except Jesse. While we're getting the body, he was making news."

Mayor Daley called an emergency meeting of the city council. Jesse stood before the Chicago City Council in the same bloodstained sweater he had been wearing at the scene of the assassination. He said, "This blood is on the chest and hands of those who would not have welcomed him here yesterday."

The speech was dramatic and moving, but SCLC aides were angry when they saw Jesse on television, displaying his bloodstained sweater. They felt he was using the tragic situation to advance his own career. They argued that the blood on his clothes could not have been Dr. King's.

Where the blood on his sweater came from and why he went back to Chicago has been argued for two decades. What Jesse did when he got there is a matter of record.

Chicago and other cities were burning. Violence was everywhere. Nine people were dead — all black — and Mayor Daley had ordered that police officers shoot to kill any rioter.

Jesse addressed 4,000 people who had come to Breadbasket headquarters. He called for peace. He pleaded for calm. He used the media to get the

Mules draw the caisson carrying the casket with the body of Dr. Martin Luther King, Jr. Jesse Jackson, upper left.

message out. "I am calling for nonviolence in the homes," he said, "on the streets, in the classrooms, and in our relationships, one to another. I'm challenging the youth today to be nonviolent as the greatest expression of faith they can make in Dr. King — to put your rocks down, put your battles down." While SCLC's high council refused to make a comment, Jesse was trying to stop the senseless death and destruction.

Critics of his behavior also forget that he, too, had lost a dear friend — one whom he had loved as a father. More than anything he did not want to see Dr. King's dream die. All things considered, Jesse's actions were more in keeping with Dr. King's nonviolent philosophy than the inaction of others.

King's death left the civil rights movement without a leader. Who would take the movement forward? Ralph Abernathy became the new head of SCLC. But Jesse's personality was in direct conflict with his. Abernathy had his way of running things, and Jesse had his own ideas. Abernathy did not relate to the younger, more impatient generation. But Jesse was appealing to them. The press liked him, too, because he was exciting and expressive.

In June 1968, Jesse was ordained a minister by the Reverends C. L. Franklin (Aretha Franklin's father) and Clay Evans. From then on, people affectionately called him Rev. Jesse. He still likes to call himself "a country preacher."

Jesse worked hard as the director of Breadbasket, working sometimes sixteen hours a day or more. But he wanted to develop and expand the project. Even when he was hospitalized for exhaustion, he continued to work. In fact, he got the idea for "Black Christmas" while in the hospital.

Black Christmas was an idea that had surprising results. With less than a month to plan it, Jesse was able to get black shoppers to "buy black" during the 1968 Christmas season. He also encouraged them to open savings accounts in black-owned banks. Children were also treated to a visit from a new Santa image, called Black Soul Saint.

Part of Jackson's brilliance as a leader has been

credited to his ability to motivate people. Biographer Barbara Reynolds stated, "It is interesting to note how Jackson pulls his events off. At three o'clock in the morning he may be hit by a new idea. When that happens, he spends the rest of the morning waking up everybody else in town who can help him pull off his brainchild."

Unfortunately, Jesse got into trouble by not tending to the financial details of his organizations, and questions of mismanagement have troubled his leadership image for years. It began with the Black Expo venture.

Building on a 1967 fair called the Operation Breadbasket Business Seminar and Exposition, and the success of Black Christmas, Jesse planned Black Expo. It was a business and entertainment fair. Held in Chicago's Amphitheater, people came from all over the country to discuss business deals, to make plans for future programs, and to share ideas. It helped young blacks set goals that went beyond the narrow limitations of the ghettos in which they lived.

Ms. Hermia Ross, the twenty-four-year-old vice president of Alpha Janitorial Supply Company, Inc., told a reporter, "I never would have thought of going into business if I hadn't seen the example at Black Expo."

The business extravaganza became an annual event and was considered to be the largest demonstration of African-American talent and success in the world. But in 1971 the Expo was marred by a financial scandal that took years to be cleared up. Innuendos of mismanagement still bother Jackson today. Briefly, this is what happened. After an audit was made, the amount taken in during the six days of the fair was $500,270.17. But newspaper reports showed that over 700,000 people attended the fair. It cost $1.50 admission, and the nightly concerts were $4.00. Simple mathematics showed that the figures were out of line.

The IRS conducted a lengthy and involved investigation of Breadbasket and Expo records. The most damaging part of the report was that the organizations' record-keeping and financial management were inept; however, there were no charges of misconduct brought against anyone.

A black power handshake is explained to Chicago's Mayor Daley at the opening breakfast of Black Expo.

One theory regarding the disputed amount of money suggests that it never existed. The attendance figures were exaggerated to make Expo look more successful.

There are very few people who believe Jackson allowed anyone to take any money but the incident did somewhat damage his credibility in the eyes of the public and especially with SCLC.

Abernathy was reportedly furious. Jesse was viewed as a renegade and top SCLC officials called for his resignation. In spite of his troubles, however, Jesse's star was rising. People listened to him. They wanted to follow him. In the November issue of a national magazine, Jesse was called, "the fiery heir apparent to Martin Luther King. . . ." And he used this growing popularity to his advantage. On December 12, 1971, Jesse Jackson resigned from SCLC. It was time for him to leave.

7
People United

In a typically dramatic move, Jesse chose Christmas Day 1971 to launch People United to Serve Humanity (PUSH). The press announcement stated that the civil rights movement had made social changes possible in the 1950s and 1960s, but as Jackson explained, "economic rights are the fundamental issues of the final decades of the twentieth century."

PUSH had the same goals as Breadbasket: "to get the unemployed employed, and to get those working but not making a livable wage organized." Jesse called it the "Civil Economics Movement."

Actually, SCLC was happy to be rid of Jesse. But soon they faced the reality that without Jackson's efforts, Breadbasket was losing ground. Abernathy named Noah Robinson, Jr., Jesse's half brother, as director of Operation Breadbasket, and Rev. John Thurston was appointed president of the Chicago chapter.

On April 10, 1972, Noah announced, "Ours will be a seven-day-a-week program rather than a once-a-week-Saturday-morning-production. . . ." Noah decided to hold Saturday morning meetings at the same time Jesse held his. It was an ill-advised decision, based, no doubt, on the competition that existed between the half brothers. SCLC was beginning to regret their decision. Noah was as unpredictable as Jesse.

Noah's campaign was not successful. He could never get the support he needed. SCLC leadership was relieved when he resigned. After that, Breadbasket was ineffective.

Meanwhile, Jesse never skipped a beat. His program moved ahead full force. By using the economic boycott as a threat, he was able to negotiate agreements with companies like Coca-Cola, Anheuser-Busch, Burger King, Avon, Quaker Oats, General Foods, and Southland Corporation to hire blacks. He expanded the program to include Hispanics and women, too.

Based on the values Jesse had learned in early childhood, he believed self-respect was the key to mental, physical, and spiritual health and happiness. People who feel good about themselves ideally will care about others and want to help others. Jesse took this basic message to cathedrals, temples, mosques, and storefronts. From classrooms to auditoriums, he talked about self-improvement.

"There is nothing more powerful than a mind made up," he said. "Make up your mind to do better, and you will."

Jesse's major asset was his command of language. When he was a teenager growing up in Greenville, he knew when to use slang and when to use standard English. He easily shifted his language pattern when speaking, so that even today he can communicate with both street gangs and heads of state effectively. For him there is no right or wrong language, just different ways of communicating an idea.

Jesse had a message he wanted to send to students. He was angered and disappointed to see the condition of inner city schools. The buildings were in poor shape. Students took drugs, carried weapons, and were members of gangs. When he saw students smoking marijuana on school grounds, it saddened him. He took PUSH into the schools with a program called PUSH for Excellence (PUSH-Excel).

Sometimes Jesse was warned that the hard-core students he came to see would be rude and noisy during assembly programs. But when Jesse spoke they listened. He wasn't soft, either. He told them, "You've got to help yourself." He shared his own childhood with them and passed on Grandmother Tibby's timeless philosophy: "You can be anything you want to be, if you try hard. . . . Don't buy what you want and beg for what you need. . . . Do for yourself. . . . Stop blaming others for what you do to yourself. Pick yourself up. You are somebody.

Jesse Jackson, leading a protest march, saying the movement for civil rights had shifted to one for "silver rights" or economic rights.

. . . I love you. God loves you. . . . You can do, if you *will* do. . . ." Thunderous applause always followed.

Then Jesse talked to the teachers, counselors, and principals and told them to follow up once he was gone. "They [the students] could bloom like flowers in the desert," he said.

At a time when young people were dropping out, Jesse was calling for them to "drop in on life." His influence was widespread because he was sincere and honest. He "spoke their language." One of his biographers said, "He has been the father figure that many of them never had, with a message that they could understand. He has also placed some of the responsibility of their lives on them. Jackson, himself a father . . . , seems to know and like these students, and this feeling has come across to the audience."

With Jesse at the helm, PUSH grew quickly. By 1972 there were chapters in sixteen cities, with over 60,000 members. Once again he worked long hours and expanded the program to include African affairs. In 1972, he headed a delegation of African-American businessmen to Monrovia, Liberia. Their purpose was to open up markets for black American-made products in that country and vice versa. Since Liberia was a nation settled by former American slaves who had returned to

John H. Johnson, publisher, and Bill Cosby with Jesse Jackson at a benefit for Operation Push.

Africa, Jackson believed the contact was historically significant. The late President Tubman of Liberia was a great-great grandson of Harriet Tubman, the slave who freed herself and returned to Southern states to help other runaways.

PUSH for Excellence (PUSH-Excel), the educational arm of Operation PUSH, included tutoring, parenting, community/school involvement, nutrition, and health activities.

Health has always been an important issue for Jackson. He has a hereditary blood disorder known as sickle cell anemia *trait*. In the late 1960s the public didn't know much about sickle cell anemia, except that it occurred most often among people of African descent. Jackson became one of the leading advocates of sickle cell anemia education and research.

When a person's red blood cells are shaped like little sickles he or she has either the *trait* or the *disease*. Those with the disease suffer from serious health problems such as extreme joint pain, high fever, dizziness, and blindness. There is no cure for either the trait or the disease, but there are medicines to help control some of the symptoms.

Those who have the trait, like Jesse, have a mixture of normal and sickle-shaped blood cells, but it is in no way life-threatening or a major health problem. In fact, persons with the trait may not be aware that they have it, because no symptoms may appear. However, if both parents have the trait, the child will probably have the full-blown disease. That is why Jesse encouraged young blacks to test for sickle cell trait before parenting children. The results have been positive. With good education and blood testing, the rate of sickle cell anemia among blacks has dropped.

As PUSH grew, so did Jesse's reputation. In his no-nonsense approach during interviews, he managed to win friends and create enemies as well. For example, he resisted being called a *black leader*. "When they refer to us as black leaders," he said on nationwide television, "they are not describing our skin color . . . they are defining our domain. When people can define you, they can confine you." He didn't want to be called a *civil rights* leader, either. His work went beyond civil rights. Labels are limiting, and clearly, Jesse Jackson was not a man who could be limited. That message was received with mixed reactions.

8
We Must Act,
Not Just React

The first time Jesse Jackson ran for public office, he was thirty years old. He ran for mayor of Chicago against Richard Daley and lost by a wide margin. But Jackson called it a victory for two reasons.

First, he was able to register thousands of new black voters. With a black candidate running, blacks were more likely to register and vote. He was right. Even though Jesse lost the election, he was sure the thousands of new voters could and would sway future Chicago campaigns.

The second advantage of Jackson's candidacy was purely psychological. No minority had ever dared to challenge the Daley political machine. Jesse did, and the spell was broken. Now the way was open for a black to run for mayor of Chicago and win.

Jackson continued to challenge Daley. At the 1972 Democratic National Convention, the rules were specific. The delegates had to be selected in open meetings. No party money or resources were to favor one candidate over another, and the party had to assure fair representation of minorities as delegates in proportion to their presence in the population. Mayor Daley ignored the rules and selected Illinois delegates in secret. Very few blacks were included.

Jesse took the case before the Democratic National Convention Credentials Commission, and the mayor's delegates were dismissed. An open election was held and a new slate was elected. It was another major political victory for Jesse.

In 1976 Mayor Daley died, and an era in political history died with him. Then, Jane Byrne became the first woman to be elected mayor of Chicago, and in 1984 Harold Washington was the first black to become mayor of Chicago.

At the twentieth anniversary of the March on Washington, in which Martin Luther King, Jr., made his "I Have a Dream" speech, Jesse stated, "Twenty years ago we came . . . to demand our freedom. Twenty years later, we have our freedom — our civil rights. But twenty years later, we still do not have equality. We have moved in. Now we must move up."

The Reagan administration had not made any

advancements in the area of civil rights. In fact, Jesse accused Reagan of being "a turn-back-the-clock" president. Jesse also warned the Democratic party that they should not take African-Americans for granted. As early as 1978, Rev. Jackson, speaking to the Republican National Committee, had said: "The Democrats have no incentive to register us because we already comprise one fourth of their total vote, and they are afraid we will vote black. The Republicans feel they have no incentive to register blacks because we tend to vote Democrat. . . . Blacks vote as intelligently and as diversely as any other group. We vote our vested interest, and only when we are ignored or when race is brought into a campaign as an issue does the black vote polarize."

There had been rumors that Jesse himself might run for president. Everywhere he went, people cheered and called out, "Run, Jesse, Run!" Bumper stickers, posters, and buttons captured the spirit of those who supported him. "Run, Jesse, Run!"

On November 3, 1983, in Washington, D.C., Jesse Jackson announced that he would seek the Democratic nomination for the presidency of the United States. (He was not the first black to seek the office. In 1972, New York Democratic congresswoman Shirley Chisholm ran for president.)

The response was mixed. Almost from the start, Jesse's campaign was considered hopeless. He was either too radical, too inexperienced, too unpredictable, or too . . . anything to be president. The most frequent excuse given was "Not yet. Maybe

Jesse with Shirley Chisholm after he announced his candidacy for the 1984 Democratic presidential nomination.

one day a black will be president." To which Jesse answered, "If not me, who? If not now, when?"

The keystone to Jesse's 1984 campaign was "The Rainbow Coalition." It consisted of whites, Native Americans, women, the poor, Hispanics, Asian-Americans, and African-Americans — all those he said had been neglected or forgotten by the Reagan administration.

He appealed to Midwestern farmers as well as urban factory workers. He supported women's rights, rights for the disabled, the elimination of discrimination, and sanctions against South Africa. He supported a Palestinian state and opposed U.S. aid to the Contras in Nicaragua. These were

61

unpopular positions among some Democrats and especially among conservative Republicans. Jesse also used his candidacy to encourage black voters to register.

A major criticism was Jesse's foreign policy, or the lack of one. But since the early 1970s, Jesse had made countless trips to Africa, Europe, the Middle East, and South America.

In January 1984, Jesse proved he was capable of negotiating with a difficult foreign power. Navy lieutenant Robert Goodman, Jr., had been shot down over Syria in 1983. He was being held as a

Lt. Robert Goodman, Jr., and Jesse Jackson at Andrews Air Force Base in Maryland.

prisoner of war. Jesse announced that he was going to Syria to seek Lieutenant Goodman's release.

The State Department didn't want him to go, and the press accused him of meddling in affairs best left to "others." The trip was written off as a publicity stunt, and nothing was expected to come of it.

Jesse and a group of fourteen African-Americans went to Syria. Jesse negotiated with Syrian president Assad for the release of Lieutenant Goodman. In *The Road to Damascus*, the Rev. Wyatt "Tee" Walker describes the announcement. "The interpreter continued . . . 'President Assad has asked me to inform you that on the basis of your moral appeal, we shall release to you Lieutenant Goodman. . . .'" According to those who were there, it seemed that Jesse Jackson had "accomplished the impossible."

At 11:30 A.M., January 3, 1984, Lieutenant Goodman was a free man. President Ronald Reagan honored both Goodman and Jackson at a White House reception.

A controversial tour of the Middle East in 1979 — which included Israel — drew fire from many American Jews. They were concerned about Jesse's support for a Palestinian state. He was photographed with Palestine Liberation Organization (P.L.O.) chairman Yasir Arafat. Jesse defended his views by saying that human rights belonged to all people.

This, along with the Goodman release, led some

Above, Jesse with Jerusalem mayor Teddy Kollek in Jerusalem, 1979. Below, Jesse presents Egyptian president Anwar Sadat with a book by Martin Luther King, Jr., Cairo, 1979.

Americans to believe that Jesse might be a danger to Israel's security. Although Jesse denied it, there was tension mounting between him and the Jewish community.

Then, while speaking privately to an individual, Jesse used the term "Hymietown" to describe New York. A reporter who overheard the conversation revealed it in *The Washington Post*. Louis Farrakhan, Chicago-based leader of the Black Muslims, sent a veiled threat to Milton Coleman, the *Post* reporter. Farrakhan also made negative comments about the Jewish religion. Jesse apologized for making his own comment, and he denounced Farrakhan's statements. But Jesse would not condemn Farrakhan as a man. The whole situation cast a cloud over the Jackson campaign.

Yet against great odds — and over 316 death threats — Jesse won Democratic primaries in four states and the District of Columbia. With no television ads and a budget of less than $6.4 million, he won 3.5 million primary and caucus votes — 465.5 delegates, 11% of the total — and came in third among the eight original candidates. He also helped to register 2 million new voters.

His speech during the Democratic Convention in San Francisco was given on prime time national television. It had the largest audience of any speech at the convention. On July 17, 1984, Jesse wowed the convention and the nation with a speech that will be, in years to come, considered a political classic. These are a few of the things he said:

"My constituency [the people he represents] *are the damned, the disinherited, the disrespected, and the despised. They are restless and seek relief. They've voted in record numbers. They have invested faith, hope, and trust in us. The Democratic party must send them a signal that we care. I pledge my best not to let them down."*

He publicly apologized to Jews for his remark, saying:

"If, in my low moments, in word, deed, or attitude, through some error of temper, taste, or tone, I have caused anyone discomfort, created pain, or revived someone's fears, that was not my truest self. If there were occasions when my grape turned into a raisin and my joybell lost its resonance, please forgive me. Charge it to my head and not my heart. My head is so limited in its attitude, but my heart is boundless in its love for the human family. I am not a perfect servant. I am a public servant, doing my best against the odds. As I grow, develop, and serve, be patient. God is not finished with me yet."

In conclusion he stated:

"No mountain is too high, no valley is too low; no forest is too dense, and no water is too deep — if your mind is made up. With eyesight,

you can see misery. But with insight, you can see the brighter side.

"Suffering breeds character, character breeds faith, and in the end, faith will not disappoint. . . ."

He was given a standing ovation. People cheered and cried at the same time. It was a moving experience for all who heard him.

But it did not translate into a victory for the Democrats in November. Walter Mondale and his running mate, Geraldine Ferraro, could not overcome Ronald Reagan's popularity. Reagan won by a landslide.

One young reporter on his first assignment asked Jesse what his plans were after the 1984 election. Jesse was tired and weary. He shocked the young reporter by answering, "No comment." It had to be a first.

9
The Challenge Goes On

After the 1984 election, Jesse continued speaking out about the issues he felt were important. Even if his views were unpopular and considered out of style, he did not turn away from his commitments. Better housing, better schools, better health care for the elderly and disadvantaged were still emphasized in his messages. "We must fight for equity, ethics, and excellence because it is the only way that we can catch up and close the gap. Those of us who are behind must run faster because we are behind in a race for educational and economic equity and parity."

He encouraged his Rainbow Coalition to vote for candidates who had their interests at heart. That was one way to catch up.

Through his PUSH program, Jesse continued to

work with young people. Like a loving father he talked to them. "Boys can make a baby," he said. Then getting straight to the point, he added, "Taking care of that baby, providing love and family stability is what makes you a man." And though he never withdrew his support from young, unwed mothers, he cautioned teenage girls to act responsibly. Usually this frank talk caused a few nervous giggles, but the message was serious and they knew it. Teenage pregnancy was at a record high in 1985. Somebody needed to do something other than point out the problem. The same applied to drugs.

Startling statistics showed that in 1986, cocaine

Jesse greeting the teenagers he is always concerned with.

use was widespread. It was no longer confined to the streets and back alleys of urban slums, but had reached the board rooms of major corporations.

While the fight against drugs was a new interest for some, it had been a Jackson concern for years.

When he spoke to the nation's youth about drugs, he asked them to consider why they call it "DOPE!" "You don't have to take drugs," he told a St. Louis audience. "You make the choice . . . so why not choose life over death?"

Standing before a room of teens in Florida, he used the "call and response" technique that has become his hallmark.

"Repeat this," he said. "My mind is a pearl . . . I can learn anything in the world. . . . Down with Dope. Up with Hope!" The national "Just say no" anti-drug campaign is based on this model of personal responsibility.

In May 1985, Western European countries organized a series of events to celebrate the fortieth anniversary of the end of World War II. President Ronald Reagan spoke to the European Parliament and visited a cemetery in Bitburg, Germany, where Nazi S.S. troopers were buried. This offended many Jews and non-Jews alike.

In the spirit of his international concerns, Jesse visited Europe at the same time. He addressed the European Parliament, too and was the principal speaker at a major peace rally in West Berlin. Jackson went to a former Nazi concentration camp. He said there, "Today the source and scope of death in this war makes us tremble. . . . The scenes of historical shame stand as landmarks that should remind us of humankind's low moments. We must remember lest we forget. This generation cannot resurrect the dead of 1945, but it can save the living in 1985. We must roll the stone away and forward. Yesterday it was Nazism and slave camps. Today it is apartheid in South Africa and missile deployment in Europe that reduce the planet to a death camp. . . ."

Educating the public about apartheid in South Africa and the involvement of American businesses in that country was also a Jackson priority.

Jesse marches through the streets of London in an anti-apartheid rally against South Africa.

Jesse Jackson comforts a Haitian refugee in Miami.

Joining with the efforts of many who oppose apartheid, Congress passed a resolution imposing sanctions against South Africa on September 29, 1986. Many major U.S. companies have stopped doing business with that country.

Everything he did between 1984 and 1987 seemed to indicate that Jesse Jackson was considering a second run for the presidency. His first campaign had made a difference. The number of African-American and Hispanic voters had had a definite impact on the 1986 elections.

In a March 1988 *Ebony* magazine article, Jesse

claimed that these new voters provided the "margin of victory for eight Southern Democratic senators, not one of whom received the majority of the white vote in his state."

As various Democrats announced their 1988 presidential candidacies, Jackson observers wondered when he would announce his. Although nothing was official, a Jackson campaign office was opened in Iowa in March 1987. Questions were asked immediately. Could Jesse win? If not, why was he running? What did he want?

His response to those same questions in 1984 applied in 1987. "Blacks, Hispanics, and the poor have always been told that they should not ask others to do for them what they can do for themselves. Thus, it would be illogical to argue that they should do everything for themselves except when it comes to running for president."

10
Can Jesse Win?

In 1987 most political analysts believed the 1988 presidential race would be between Vice President George Bush and Colorado senator Gary Hart.

Although Bush had an impressive political record, there were still many unanswered questions about his knowledge of and participation in the controversial Iran-Contra affair. Hart had run well against Walter Mondale in the 1984 Democratic primaries. He was expected to win his party's nomination with little or no difficulty, and most likely go on to win the presidency in November.

Then scandal forced Senator Hart to withdraw from the race. The Democrats didn't have a strong contender. A lot of Democrats encouraged New York governor Mario Cuomo to enter the race, but he refused.

Other Democrats were interested. They were Colorado congresswoman Pat Schroeder; Missouri congressman Richard Gephardt; Michael Dukakis, governor of Massachusetts; Joseph Biden, senator from Delaware; Bruce Babbitt, former Arizona governor; Albert Gore, senator from Tennessee; Paul Simon, senator from Illinois; and Jesse Jackson.

Pat Schroeder dropped out. Then there were seven. A *Time* magazine article stated, "Of the seven, only Jesse Jackson has an established reputation, yet he has virtually no chance of winning."

Yet as early as September 4, 1987, a *Time* magazine poll showed that 80% of those queried were familiar with Jackson as opposed to 29% who knew Dukakis; 80% believed Jackson cared about the average American, and 66% stated they trusted Jackson, topped only by Dukakis with 68%. Jackson consistently ranked in the top three candidates for trustworthiness and ability to handle difficult international affairs. In polls run by *The Washington Post*, ABC/TV, and *The New York Times*, Jackson would place first at one time or another.

From the start, people saw the differences between Jesse's 1984 and 1988 campaigns. Ann Lewis, a Jackson adviser and former political director of the Democratic National Committee, said, " '84 was a crusade. This is a *real* campaign."

To see Jackson in action, to hear crowds roaring "Jesse! Jesse! Jesse!" was a unique experience. People pressed to touch him, and women thrust their babies toward him to be touched or kissed. A *Time* reporter wrote, "No one who has seen the white hands of farmers, factory workers, and the elderly straining to touch Jackson can doubt that his campaign in 1988, more so than the one in 1984, will leave America less racist than it found it."

Jackson wasn't saying anything he hadn't been saying for years, but he was saying it with more political polish. From Mississippi to Maine, Jesse spread the message of the Rainbow Coalition. And people listened. He was strong on economic justice. He called for large corporations to pay their fair share of taxes. He promised that if he was elected, he would work to institute a very strong

In 1984 Jesse spread the message of the Rainbow Coalition, as he continued to do in his 1988 campaign.

anti drug program, better education, less military spending, a more active role in Middle East peace negotiations, and a hard-line position against South African apartheid.

"Oppression is too great a thing to war alone," was his standard summary. Standing before crowds of white farmers, black laborers, senior citizens, and jobless youth, he attacked the Reagan administration for ignoring their needs. "Together," he said, his eyes flashing, "we can change the course of the nation." People were stirred when they heard him. Large crowds gathered wherever he went in Iowa, New Hampshire, Mississippi, Missouri, and Maine, from coast to coast, border to border.

Jesse also wanted to see changes made inside the Democratic party. He called for the leadership to "include people rather than exclude them." The poor, minorities, and women should not be forgotten by the Democratic party, because traditionally they had been the party's most loyal voters. He wanted issues that concerned this portion of the Democratic party to be addressed — unemployment, runaway national debt, slums, drugs, hunger, the homeless, AIDS, and apartheid.

In 1984 Jesse's positions might have seemed out of the mainstream of American politics. But he was not the only person aware that the economic recovery the Reagan administration boasted about had missed a lot of people. In his announcement speech in October 1987, George Bush had stated, "I want a prosperity that stays, that broadens, that deepens, and that touches, finally, all Americans. . . ."

Jackson repeatedly warned the Democratic party that the Rainbow Coalition was a powerful voting block that should not be overlooked or taken for granted.

Campaigning long, hard hours seemed not to affect Jesse. His days began at dawn and sometimes didn't end until the next dawn. Sometimes he caught only a catnap between flights from one city to another. All he needed was a gentle shaking and he was wide awake, fresh, and ready to go, even though he might have had only four hours' sleep in the previous forty-eight. But his efforts were paying off in the voting booths.

Richard Gephardt won the first primary in Iowa, but his campaign seemed to lose steam soon after. Michael Dukakis and Albert Gore emerged as the two front-runners. And Jesse? He was consistently ranking second or third in each primary.

On Super Tuesday, March 8, 1988, twenty Southern states held primary elections, which resulted in three front-runners: Gore, Jackson, and Dukakis. Analysts quickly explained that Jackson's phenomenal showing was due to the heavy black population in Southern states. The center of the Rainbow Coalition — minorities, women, and the poor — was in the South. The Michigan primary shattered that argument.

Jackson won Detroit with a landslide, as was expected. But he surprised everyone when the re-

Presidential candidate Jackson at breakfast with the Becker family after spending the night in their Cudhay, Wisconsin, home.

sults from predominantly white areas like Kalamazoo, Saginaw, and Ann Arbor came in. Jesse won 54% of the vote as opposed to Dukakis's 29%. The statewide tally showed that Jackson received more votes than any of the other contenders. He now had 646 delegates; Dukakis had 653, and Gore was a distant third with 381.

The press maintained that even though Jesse had won, he was still "unelectable." Ann Lewis summed up the anger and frustration that some African-Americans felt about the analysis. "A white man of Jackson's age, talent, energy, and interests would almost surely have gathered governmental credentials by this stage of his career."

79

All spring, kitchen table debates included the question, "Can Jesse win?" He was one of the top three candidates, yet he was still considered "unelectable." Nobody wanted to admit that racism was the reason. Other reasons were given. He had not been elected to any public office. He didn't have governmental experience. He was still considered too radical.

But polls showed that the country was not ready for a black president or a black vice president, whether it was Jesse or some other candidate. It was not his lack of experience or even his ideas that made Jesse Jackson "unelectable." He was black — that was the real reason.

A *New York Times* poll showed that 39% of the people questioned would not vote for Jackson because of his lack of experience. But 32% said they would not vote for him or any other black candidate; only 12% said they did not like his ideas.

With Dukakis and Jackson running neck and neck, the candidates headed for the April 19, 1988, showdown in New York, where Jackson was strongly opposed by New York City mayor Ed Koch.

Jesse's position on the Middle East wasn't popular in 1984, but in 1988, his statements did not seem so far off center. "The Israelis and the Palestinians are in a death grip," he said. "They have their arms around each other and a knife at each other's back . . . afraid to let go."

An Israeli journalist wrote: "Israel and its friends

in the American Jewish community clearly have an important self-interest in establishing as decent a relationship with him [Jackson] as possible."

Overcoming the unfortunate "Hymietown" remark, Jackson won an impressive number of votes in the New York primary, coming in ahead of Mayor Koch's choice, Al Gore.

The June 7, 1988, primary races in California, New Jersey, Montana, and New Mexico ended the long and tiring primary season. Jesse had finished in second place. Overall he had won an impressive 7 million votes during the primaries. Michael Dukakis was the Democratic winner. Yet most Amer-

Presidential hopeful Jackson with his children after voting in the Illinois primary. The children, from left to right, are Santita, Jonathan, and Jesse, Jr.

icans didn't know who he was or what he stood for. Jesse was clearly a force the Democratic party had to deal with.

On the Republican side, George Bush was the unchallenged winner. Senator Robert Dole, Congressman Jack Kemp, General Alexander Haig, and television evangelist Pat Robertson had, at various times, been in the race. The Democrats were scheduled to meet in Atlanta to formalize their nomination. The Republicans were going to convene in New Orleans in August.

The weeks before the conventions were filled with guessing and supposing. Would Jackson accept the nomination for vice president? Some thought he might be asked and then turn it down graciously. He didn't want to be a scapegoat for a Democratic loss. "What does Jesse want — the vice presidency, an ambassadorship, secretary of state?" Jesse answered as the true politician that he is: "a better America."

11
Jesse Can't Lose

Michael Dukakis was the Democratic candidate for president, and the country watched and waited to see how he would handle Jesse Jackson. The black community hoped Jesse Jackson would be the first African-American to be honored with the *offer* of a vice presidential candidacy. One California delegate, a member of the Rainbow Coalition, said what most African-Americans were thinking. "If Jesse were white, there would be no debate whatsoever. He'd be the vice presidential candidate."

The Dukakis organization selected Texas senator Lloyd Bentsen as the nominee for vice president, and Jesse was neither consulted nor told before the public announcement was made. *The*

New York Times summarized the Bentsen selection as a "good choice, bad handling."

Jesse responded angrily. He was accused by some of his own party members of being a "spoiler," and a "sore loser." Dukakis's move, in Jackson's opinion, was insensitive and much like the old slave/master relationships. "It is too much to expect that I will go out in the field and be the champion vote picker and bale them up and bring them back to the big house and get a reward of thanks while people who do not pick nearly as much votes, who don't carry the same amount of weight among the people, sit in the big house and make the decisions."

Dukakis's team explained that they had tried to contact Jackson before the official announcement was made. Jackson responded, "The issue . . . is not about the time of a call. It is not about a recommendation for a running mate. It is about . . . a relationship based on shared responsibility."

Dukakis was angered by Jackson's attitude. He fired back that on a football team, there was only room for one quarterback, not two. Given Jesse's college experience at the University of Illinois, that was not the best example for Dukakis to use.

There was obvious tension between Jackson and Dukakis. The weeks before the convention were spent trying to patch up the hard feelings between them. It was arranged for the two families to celebrate the Fourth of July together. It was an uncomfortable situation for the men, but their wives seemed to like each other very much.

Finally Jackson and Dukakis met to discuss *real* issues. Their open discussion led to a workable truce. To everyone's relief, the convention opened with a unified Democratic party.

Former president Jimmy Carter commented that it was the "first time . . . we've seen a potential showdown between a black leader and a white leader in the primary season. . . . I think what Jesse has done in his extraordinary campaign is to let moderate and even many conservative Democrats see that the issues . . . apply to them." It was history in the making.

The Democrats put forth a lot of effort to showcase their differences and their unity. Their pro-

Jesse Jackson and Michael Dukakis in a show of unity.

gram was centered around family and ethnic culture. Michael Dukakis was of Greek heritage. Jesse was of African-American roots.

There was also a theme of "the new generation" coming to the forefront of American politics. An appearance by young John F. Kennedy, Jr., who introduced his uncle, Senator Ted Kennedy, was a glimpse at the past and the future. Also in attendance was Martin Luther King III, son of Martin Luther King, Jr., and Joseph P. Kennedy, son of assassinated senator Robert F. Kennedy.

Jesse Jackson was introduced by his five children, who dazzled spectators with their poise and dignity. Twelve-year-old Jacqueline, the youngest of the Jackson children began, "If I could vote, I'd vote for my dad."

Yusef, age seventeen, addressed a concern shared by his peers. "Many members of my generation have tried to spell relief D-R-U-G-S. . . ." Santita and Jonathan were followed by Jesse, Jr., the son many feel will follow in his father's political footsteps.

With typical Jackson eloquence, Jesse, Jr., stated, "I am sure that the children in the King family are proud to be Kings. And I'm sure that the children in the Kennedy family are proud to be Kennedys. But we, the children of Jesse and Jacqueline Jackson, are proud to be Jacksons. . . . A new generation — my generation — is coming. We have not given up the dream."

When the young man ended by calling his father to the convention floor, the crowd went wild. Applause shook the auditorium. Jackson delegates wept and cheered and jumped for joy. They marched and threw confetti.

For Jesse it was a moment of personal triumph. He had overcome a lot of criticism, and scratched and clawed every step of the way to that podium. All the small-town gossip, race hatred, and petty arguments were behind him. There was no doubt Jesse understood the historical importance of that evening. And he was ready.

Appearing confident and self-assured, he calmly looked to his left and to his right as though acknowledging some unseen presence. Perhaps he was aware of the invisible men and women upon

Jesse Jackson addresses the Democratic National Convention, Atlanta, July 19, 1988.

whose shoulders he was standing — the rebellious slave Nat Turner, the great abolitionist and orator Frederick Douglass, labor leader A. Philip Randolph, First Lady Eleanor Roosevelt, Chief Justice Earl Warren, Martin Luther King, Jr., to name a few.

Jesse Jackson delivered a masterful speech that has been called brilliant. He began by saluting Dukakis and saying, "His foreparents came to America on immigrant ships. My foreparents came to America on slave ships. But whatever the original ships, we are both in the same boat now."

Jesse acknowledged his parents and grandmother, and touched every heart when for fifty minutes he spoke with compassion and concern about those issues for which he had fought so long and hard.

Part of his speech was a beautiful story about his grandmother's quilt. He told the story to explain simply the Rainbow Coalition idea. Grandmother Tibby took pieces of fabric, some of them old, some from raggedy and useless material. With loving hands she stitched the pieces together — some red, some brown, some yellow, some black, some white. Sleeping under the blanket always kept him warm and made him feel loved and safe.

Then he told his listeners that like the pieces in the quilt they were not strong alone. "Your patch ain't big enough," he said. Then returning to his familiar theme he added, "Together we can make a difference."

When he finished there was a moment of silence.

Jesse and his family.

The audience seemed to be spellbound. Then thunderous applause followed. It was impossible to hear over the noise. President Carter said Jackson's speech was "the best ever given at a convention, certainly in my lifetime. I don't think he is equaled anywhere as an orator."

The following night it was Governor Dukakis's turn. Could he, who was not known for being a dynamic speaker, overcome Jackson's presence? Introduced by his Academy-Award-winning cousin, Olympia Dukakis, "The Duke" gave "the speech of his career." He began by praising all five of the Jackson children. He singled out Jesse's twelve-year-old daughter, saying, "Young Jacqueline Jackson goes to school in my state, and last month she visited with me at the statehouse in Boston. She's a remarkable young woman and I know her parents are very, very proud of her." Indeed they were. Jackie stood and took a graceful bow. As the camera panned to where Jesse and Jacqueline Jackson were seated, they both were beaming.

The Democratic Convention ended on an up beat. Candidate Dukakis seemed almost a certain

Michael and Kitty Dukakis, Jackie and Jesse Jackson, and Beryl Ann and Lloyd Bentsen at the Democratic National Convention.

winner in November. The polls had him leading Bush by a wide margin.

In August, the Republican Convention was held in New Orleans. As expected, it was organized, orderly, and unified. Then Bush named Indiana senator Dan Quayle as his running mate. The Republican mainstream was not impressed with Quayle. They wondered why Bush did not pick from other, more prominent, Republicans like Congressman Kemp or Senator Dole. But the vice president held firm and the Bush-Quayle ticket was nominated.

Bush also gave a memorable acceptance speech. In a rare moment of eloquence he stated, "I wonder sometimes if we have forgotten who we are. But we're the people who sundered a nation rather than allow a sin called slavery — we're the people who rose from the ghettos and deserts. . . . But where is it written that we must act as if we do not care, as if we are not moved? Well, I am moved. I want a kinder, gentler nation."

But the 1988 campaign was neither kind nor gentle, and was considered by many to be the "most ruthless and useless" in recent history. Bush won the election in November by a large margin. Despite the low voter turnout, Democrats did well in state and local elections, but the top job eluded them for the third time since 1980.

Although Jesse went on the stump for candidates all over the country, many felt the Rainbow Coalition had lost its appeal after the convention and didn't work for Dukakis. But Jesse continued to actively campaign for local and state candidates, and most benefited from his support. What happened? Political analysts will be writing and debating it for years. As for Jesse Jackson, the day after Bush won, he was asked what his future plans were. He answered, "We start campaigning for 1992 tomorrow!"

12
Proud to Be a Jackson

The 1988 election ended, but Jesse didn't seem to notice. After a few weeks' rest, he continued his exhaustive schedule of meetings, speaking engagements, and conferences. The work of Operation PUSH, PUSH Foundation, and PUSH-Excel goes on. The day-to-day operations are handled by a well-trained and experienced staff. The Rainbow Coalition, formed after the 1984 election, is headquartered in Washington, D.C., and it has become the hub of Jackson's political organization. Whenever Jesse is in Chicago he still conducts his Saturday morning services, still calling himself a "country preacher."

Jesse Jackson has always been in the public eye, but his family has not. Jackie Jackson is the family

Jesse receives a kiss from eight-year-old Jacqueline, 1984.

anchor. A petite 5'1", and weighing less than 108 pounds, she is very self-assured and articulate. She has always made the family's two-story Tudor-style house on Chicago's South Side a comfortable home, a peaceful place away from the hustle and hurry of public life. Whether making kitchen curtains, entertaining an international leader, or accompanying Jesse on the campaign trail, Jackie Jackson is her own person who has an interesting and fulfilling life outside the shadow of her famous husband. "Don't box me in to any one function," she told a reporter.

Jackie admits that she misses Jesse when he is gone, but she considers her husband of many years a good friend. "Jesse is rarely home," she says. "He returns because he wants to and when he does, I am happy to have him back." The threats on her husband's life worry her. "I'm never relaxed when he's gone. And I can't say that I'm unafraid, but I have disciplined myself to function while I am fearful."

Discipline seems to be the key to the way the Jacksons have reared their children. When his five children were growing up, Jesse spent "good" time with them. They enjoyed playing basketball together and talking openly about what had been happening while he was away. He always wanted a full report. On the *Donahue* show, Jesse, Jr., affectionately called "Fella" by his family, praised his parents for being strict, but always loving and caring.

Daughter Santita, 25 and the oldest of the Jackson children, attended Howard University in Washington, D.C. She turned down an offer to attend Harvard because during an admissions interview she was harshly questioned about her father's political positions. She worked as a legislative aide for Representative Gus Savage, Democrat from Illinois, but took a leave and is singing on tour with Roberta Flack.

Twenty-two-year-old Jonathan Luther Jackson was given Dr. King's middle name. He and his brother Jesse, Jr., age 23, recently graduated from North Carolina A&T. Both sons are interested in working with their father. Jesse, Jr., is an at-large member of the Democratic National Committee

(DNC) and attends Chicago Theological Seminary. Jonathan is pursuing an MBA degree and is president of a family business.

The three older children remember attending boycotts, civil rights protests, and peace marches with their parents. The two younger Jacksons do not. Yusef DuBois, whose nickname is Tootie, is attending the University of Virginia on a football scholarship, and Jacqueline is a student at Fay School outside Boston, Massachusetts. They both are proud of their father and travel with him on vacations and holidays.

Jesse Jackson does not drink, smoke, or use

Jesse, Jr., after he received his diploma from the Saint Albans National Cathedral School for Boys in Washington. Rev. Jackson gave the commencement address at the graduation, in 1984.

The Jackson family.

drugs. Although he has been accused of being an opportunist, he doesn't have a lot of money. A careful IRS audit showed that he often overpays, rather than underpays, his taxes. His lifestyle is not extravagant, and his tastes are simple. He has shed his African dress of the 1970s, choosing instead to wear business suits. However, he has not shed his desire to bring about better understanding among all Americans. He eats in modest restaurants, buys and uses goods and services provided by black businesses. His love of good soul food is beginning to show in the extra weight he has picked up during his forties, but he remains in good physical condition. The Jacksons support black artists, sports, and all the performing arts. Good gospel singing is still a favorite of Jesse's. In many ways he really is "the country preacher."

When asked to explain his life and values, he quickly gives credit to his family. The dedication in his book *Straight From the Heart* summarizes his gratitude. "To my grandmother, Matilda, who in her lifetime will never read this book because she can neither read nor write — but who gave me encouragement to do so. To my mother, Helen Jackson, who, along with my grandmother, took me to church. To Charles Jackson, who adopted me and gave me his name, his love, his encouragement, discipline, and a high sense of self-respect — who has since gone to be with God but whose presence in my life assures me that heaven smiles upon our sincere efforts. Their love, concern, affection, sacrifice, and discipline helped, in my formative years, to shape my values."

Epilogue:
Keep Hope Alive

Jesse Louis Jackson has made a difference in American politics. He will be remembered as the first black to run for president of the United States and be taken seriously by the voters, winning a total of 1,170 primary delegates.

Professor James David Barber of Duke University, who has written several books on the presidency, says Jackson has done for African-Americans what President John F. Kennedy did for Catholics. Until Kennedy, a Catholic was considered unelectable. Until Jackson, no black person was thought electable to this high office. According to Barber, Jesse Jackson has "registered a social and cultural shift that enables us all to entertain the possibility of having a black president in this country." To an increasing number of

Americans, color is not a factor when choosing a candidate to support.

Jesse has also restored minority interest in the American political system. As one black mother said, "Jesse Jackson may not ever become president of the United States, but he made it possible for my son to run . . . and win!" Hope for the future is the Jackson legacy.

This achievement alone will secure him a place in history, but there are other areas in which Jesse Jackson has made a significant difference.

Some critics suggest that Jesse has not said anything "new or specific." But his life's work seems to suggest something different. For nearly thirty years Jesse Jackson has been a consistent voice against racism and racial discrimination. And he has done more than talk about it. Through programs sponsored by Operation Breadbasket, PUSH, and the Rainbow Coalition, minorities have gotten better jobs, better housing and health care, improved education, and a stronger voice in government. For example, Ronald H. Brown was the first American of African descent to be elected chairman of the Democratic National Committee, in 1988.

Jackson's anti-drug campaign helped set the tone for stronger legislation in the war against drugs. And his "I Am Somebody" message has motivated students to take responsibility for their lives by exercising self-control. To millions of disenfranchised people, he has made a difference by leading large voter registration drives, and without

100

exception, Jesse Jackson has been a spokesman for the outcast, the downtrodden, and the disregarded. He has also been an inspiration to his family. In May 1988, his mother-in-law, Gertrude Brown, graduated from Hampton University with a bachelor of arts degree in sociology.

"We have a great nation," he has said many times. "But it can be greater if all Americans are included." That is what he reportedly discussed with President-Elect George Bush in their December 1988 meeting. When President Bush presented his budget to Congress in February 1989, he sent a message to the nation that racism and bigotry had to be eliminated in America forever! He quoted Jesse Jackson by saying, "We must keep hope alive."

Jesse's story is not over. He will be a newsmaker for years to come. But if he should do no more than what he has done already, he has made a difference. Long ago, Grandmother Tibby told Jesse, *"Can't* got drowned in a soda bottle." So, he grew up never allowing "can't" to cripple or maim his spirit. In Jesse's pursuit of excellence, he has made many people try a little harder. And through his efforts the door of opportunity has opened for many more.

Bibliography

Books (for children)

Halliburton, Warren. *The Picture Life of Jesse Jackson*. New York: Franklin Watts, 1972.
Kosof, Anna. *Jesse Jackson*. New York: Franklin Watts, 1984.
Westman, Paul. *Jesse Jackson: I Am Somebody*. Minneapolis: Dillon Press, Inc., 1981.

Books (for adults)

Collins, Sheila D. *The Rainbow Challenge*. New York: Monthly Review Press, 1986.
Hatch, Roger D. *Beyond Opportunity — Jesse Jackson's Vision of America*. Philadelphia: Fortress Press, 1988.

102

Jackson, Rev. Jesse L. *Straight From the Heart*. Philadelphia: Fortress Press, 1987.

Landess, Thomas and Richard Quinn. *Jesse Jackson and the Politics of Race*. Ottawa, Illinois: Jameson Books, 1985.

Reed, Adolph, J., Jr. *The Jesse Jackson Phenomenon*. New Haven: Yale University Press, 1986.

Reynolds, Barbara A. *Jackson: America's David*. Washington, D.C.: JFJ Associates, 1985.

Stone, Eddie. *Jesse Jackson*. New York: Halloway House, 1984.

Walker, Wyatt Tee. *Road to Damascus*. New York: Martin Luther King Fellows Press, 1985.

Articles

Randolph, Laura B. "Can Jesse Jackson Win?" *Ebony* magazine, March 1988, pp. 154–162.

"Respect and Respectability." *Time* magazine, August 17, 1987, p. 16.

Scott, Walter. "Personality Parade." *Parade, The Sunday Newspaper Magazine*, July 10, 1988, p. 2.

St. Louis Post-Dispatch. "Jackson Youth." July 21, 1988, p. 14A.

"The Party's New Soul." *Time* magazine, July 25, 1988, p. 17.

"Unhappy Democrats, a Loyal G.O.P." *Time* magazine, September 14, 1987, p. 22.

"Proud to Be Jacksons." *Newsweek* magazine, August 1, 1988, p. 21.

The New York Times. "Jackson Is Seen as Winning a Solid Place in History." April 19, 1988, p. 10.

Index

A&P Grocery Stores, 37
Abernathy, Ralph, 29, 30, 42, 43, 44, 47, 50, 51
Africa, 55-56, 62
African-Americans, 1, 38, 48, 55, 60, 61, 63, 72, 79, 83, 86, 99, 100; (see also Blacks)
AIDS, 77
Alabama, 15, 28
Anheuser-Busch, 52
Ann Arbor, Michigan, 79
Apartheid, 71, 77
Arafat, Yasir, 63
Asian-Americans, 61
Assad, President (of Syria), 63
Atlanta, Georgia, 26, 30, 33, 82
Avon, 52

Babbitt, Bruce, 75
Baseball, 11-14, 17, 22
Basketball, 11
Bentsen, Lloyd, 83-84
Beyond Opportunity—Jesse Jackson's Vision of America, 102
Biden, Joseph, 75
Bitburg, Germany, 70
"Black Christmas," 47, 48
Black Expo, 48-49, 50
Black Muslims, 65
Black Soul Saint, 47
Blacks, boycotts by, 34-38; businesses owned and supported by, 37-38, 47, 48, 55; Democratic party and, 60-61; discrimination against in sports, 13; hiring of, 24, 35, 37-38, 52; presidency of U.S. and, 1-2, 60-61, 99-100; racial pride of, 38, 40-41; Republican party and, 60; sickle cell anemia and, 56-57; support for Jesse Jackson, 2, 35, 78;

treatment of in South, 4-6; (see also African-American)
Boycotts, 28, 34, 52, 96; resulting in employment of blacks, 35, 37-38
Brown, Gertrude, 101
Brown, Ronald H., 100
Burger King, 52
Burns, Matilda (Grandmother Tibby), 6-7, 53, 88, 98, 101
Bush, George, 1, 74, 77-78, 82, 91, 92, 101
Byrne, Jane, 59

California, 31, 81, 83
Campaign to End Slums, The, 32
Carter, Jimmy, 85, 89
Charlotte, North Carolina, 7
Chicago Daily Defender, 30
Chicago, Illinois, 25, 26, 31, 32, 33, 38, 45, 48, 52, 58-59, 65, 93; City Council, 45; riots in, 31-32, 45-46; South Side, 24, 34, 35, 94
Chicago Theological Seminary, 23, 96
Chisholm, Shirley, 60
"Civil Economics Movement," 51
Civil rights movement, 15, 17, 18-19, 20, 37, 38, 47, 51, 57, 59, 60, 96; role of black churchmen in, 23
Coca-Cola, 52
Cocaine, 69-70
Coleman, Milton, 65
Colorado, 74, 75
Concentration camps, 70, 71
Congress of Racial Equality (CORE), 18
Congress, U.S., 28, 31, 101
Constitution, U.S., 32, 72
Contras, 61, 74
Coordination Council of Community

104

call to the ministry, 20, 23; candidacy for mayor of Chicago, 58-59; childhood, 3-10; children of, 86-87, 90, 95-96; CORE and, 18; Michael Dukakis and, 83-86, 89-90; education of, 9-10, 14-20; electability of, 1-2, 79-82; family and, 8-9; Louis Farrakhan and, 65; financial mismanagement and, 48-50; foreign policy of, 62-63; Lieutenant Goodman and, 63; hospitalized, 47; "Hymietown" remark, 65-66, 81; "I Am Somebody," 40, 100; impact on American politics, 72-73, 99; Jewish Americans and, 63, 65-66, 80-81; Dr. Martin Luther King, Jr., and, 26-33, 44-47; leadership style of , 19, 30, 47-48; lifestyle of, 96-98; marriage of, 20; Middle East and, 63, 77, 80; military spending and, 77; Operation Breadbasket and, 33, 34-38; ordination of, 47; political awareness, 17; polls and, 75, 80; 1984 presidential campaign, 60-61, 65, 75; 1988 presidential campaign, 2-3, 73, 74-89; PUSH and, 51-57, 93; racial discrimination and, 5-6, 12-13, 15, 17, 100; religious influence on, 7-8; role models for, 20, 22; SCLC resignation, 50; Selma-to-Montgomery March, 28-30; sickle cell anemia and, 56-57; sit-ins and, 17-19; South Africa and, 71-72, 77; speaking skills/speeches of, 1, 7-8, 38, 40, 53, 65-67, 88-89; students and, 53-54, 100; threats on life of, 95; University of Illinois and, 14; vice presidential nomination and, 82, 83-84
Jackson, Jesse, Jr., 86, 95-96
Jackson, Jonathan Luther, 86, 95
Jackson, Santita, 86, 95

Jackson, Yusef DuBois, 86, 96
Jesse Jackson (by A. Kosof), 102
Jesse Jackson (by E. Stone), 103
Jesse Jackson and the Politics of Race, 103
Jesse Jackson: I Am Somebody, 102
Jesse Jackson Phenomenon, The, 103
Jews, 63, 65-66, 70, 80-81
Jim Crow laws, 24

Kalamazoo, Michigan, 79
Kellogg's, 34
Kemp, Jack, 82, 91
Kennedy, John F., 99
Kennedy, John F., Jr., 86
Kennedy, Joseph P., 86
Kennedy, Robert F., 86
Kennedy, Ted, 86
King, Martin Luther, Jr., 22, 23, 26-33, 40, 41, 42-47, 50, 59, 86, 88, 95; assassination of 44-47; Chicago and, 32-33; criticism and, 32; friendship with Jesse Jackson, 33, 42-43; resentment of, 32; SCLC and, 26, 28; voting laws and, 28
King, Martin Luther, III, 86
Koch, Ed, 80, 81

Liberia, 55
Looting, 31
Lorraine Motel, 42
Los Angeles, California, 31
Lunch counters, (see Sit-ins)

Maine, 76, 77
Marches, 28-29, 31, 33, 34, 96; March on Washington, 59
Marijuana, 53
Massachusetts, 75
Mathis, J.D., 11
Memphis, Tennessee, 40, 41, 42-44
Michigan, 1-2, 78-79
Middle East, 62-63, 77, 80
Militant youths, 38-39